GENTLE
SLAUGHTER

GENTLE SLAUGHTER

Philip Belcher

MadHat Press
Cheshire, Massachusetts

MadHat Press
PO Box 422, Cheshire MA 01225

Copyright © 2022 Philip Belcher
All rights reserved

The Library of Congress has assigned
this edition a Control Number of
2022943470

ISBN 978-1-952335-47-1 (paperback)

Cover image: *Virgin and Unicorn* by Domenico Zampieri (ca. 1602)
Cover design by Marc Vincenz
Book design by MadHat Press

www.MadHat-Press.com

Published in the United States of America

for
Kelly, Owen, and Kera

for
Rod and Sarah

and in memoriam
Posey, Jean, and David Belcher

Table of Contents

I
NOT QUITE SISYPHUS

Not Quite Sisyphus	3
Epitome	5
The Call	7
Exodus	8
The Vicar	9
Variations on a Theory	11
Semi-Private	12
My Groans, My Flies	13
Talking to Worms	14
Down Dog	15
CNA	16
Wick (Rome 2014)	17
January 2015	18
The Sovereign	19
Invoice	20
Gardener	22
Acoustics	23

II
SOMETHING BORROWED

Another Good Morning	27
Donnie with Baby and Cows 1999	28
Eric with Spike the Rooster 2001	30
Bird in Hand	31
Frame of Reference	32
After Hours with *The Iliad*	33
Fear of Giants	35
Kentucky Conclave	36
Some Local Cindy	38
Memoir	40
Aviary	41

III
BOY ON FIRE

Luminary	45
I Spent Most of Elementary School Fearing Quicksand	48
Elsewhere	50
Missing a Wound	52
Slur	54
The Lesson	56
Question for Heavy	57
Prelude to a Hunt	58
Otherwise Gentle	60
The Cards	61
Undressing the Dead	62
Renaissance Man	63
It's Pronounced [tree-uh n]	64
Lines on the Installation of My Brother	65
Dead of Winter	67

IV
GENTLE SLAUGHTER

Ode to the God of Dogs	71
Lines Composed in the Jim Barkley Toyota Service Department Lounge	73
Dry	76
Bait	77
Beatitude	78
In Tübingen	79
Inquisition	81
Requiem	82
Preserved	84
Blue	86
To Dr. Paulson on the Eve of Surgery	87
Reconstruction Sonnet	88
New Year, White County, Arkansas	89
Qilin	90

Bathos	92
And We Question the Will of the Sullen	93
Gentle Slaughter	95
Acknowledgments	97
About the Author	99

I
Not Quite Sisyphus

... and he thought, This is my father and I am his son, and it brought him a degree of peace.

—Robert Olmstead, *Coal Black Horse*

Not Quite Sisyphus

Bombings at the Yemen mosque
do not move him,

and the television's blare
does not distract

him from pushing the parlor's
oak desk. Leverage

is difficult from the chair.
The unlocked wheels

roll back as he accosts the
obstinate wood.

The tight grip whitens his nails.
The woman who claims

this space, who reigned here months
before he came,

screams for him to stop shoving
the furniture

in what she believes is her
den in Des Moines

but is in fact the room where
orderlies park

Philip Belcher

residents who only shriek,
digest, and blink.

My father is not deterred.
He keeps to his

striving, not quite Sisyphus,
who understood

the cause of his sentence, but
with some mute sense

that all is not as it should
be, shouldering

the myth that he can reverse
a single wrong.

Epitome

Sundays after church, after lunch,
they drove down Franklin Street

past the red brick ranch backed up
to the railroad bed. She bent toward

her son, pointed at the Ford leaking
coolant on the drive, and said in a voice

as flat as the back of her hand,
Preacher's home by two—epitome

of sloth. He nodded, leaned against
the door to dream of his own congregation:

rising tall behind the pulpit, King James
spine cracked across his raised palm.

His words and God's are one, an eagle
poised to dive and drag a shadow

over the worshippers' faces.
Now, window blinds parse sunset into bars,

and I think of Aurora, how she never
escaped the voice of Tithonus,

even as his body dried to a rind.
The boy grown old sits chained

Philip Belcher

in Parkinson's mute cell, still bearing
the weight of a judgment he cannot unhear.

The Call

If he cocks his head just right,
stills the chimes with his cane

and cups a hand behind his good ear,
the hum of trucks on Highway 3

sounds like wind in his father's trees.
Young among the peaches,

he spoke with God. He saw miracles
and the future. Flies twirled like angels

on bruised and fallen fruit. Smudge pots
blackened dusk and kept the devil freeze

at bay. He disdained his mother's dream:
bequeathing these fields, passing them

down to her sons and theirs. As if he were
a kite rising on warm air, he felt both the pull

of the possible and the farm's
anchoring tug. The voice was a braid

of his mother's and God's, and virtue
meant pleasing them both. It was good,

then, that he knew the word *sacrifice*,
how often damaged trees were burned.

Philip Belcher

Exodus

> *At dusk the soul rocks in its homesickness.*
> —Derek Walcott, "In Italy"

The six o'clock rattles the track
behind North Greenville's college farm,
blasts a cloud of grackles from the oak.

Beneath the screaming parabola
carved into dusk's yellow band,
a freshman grips his knees, leans

into the flank of his ward,
a Guernsey stooping for grass.
He warms his face against

her steaming hide and imagines
peaches hanging from his father's
trees, the smudge pots belching

dark into dark, his mother counting
crates in the shed—rocking the arm
of the adding machine—

the harvest tumbling through
the washer's hiss. He considers
the sweet smell of juice seeping

through a bruise, how distance
is gauged by more than space,
the mandatory cull of wounded fruit.

The Vicar

The trees are thick and dark near Millett,
where Mr. Price milled his grain, where his dam
organized the pond into a congregation

of bream not far from a bend in the river
called Little Hell. To their children
the locals bequeath legends of whirlpools

sucking down ski and bass boats. You would
believe them, too, if you saw the currents
colliding there, jostling for dominance

like theories of evil, undercutting the banks,
curling in lament. But beyond the cypress
soaking their twisted roots rise legions

of disciplined pines. Near the cabin
where my father fled on Fridays to rest
for Sundays, to escape the grinding politics

of church, quiet pines swept the sky.
Their needles ensured sanctuary
by quilting the sun, forbidding other plants

from taking root. Yet among them
a crippled maple grew in an open space,
spreading its crooked limbs like the arms

of Shiva caught in mid-dance. When twelve,
I named it Vicar, and I liked it there: the silent
competition of species, the absence of human

drama, the liturgy of wind and wood.
Last year I went back to Millett. The granary
is mute. A hole in the silo welcomes wrens

and rain. The headstone over Mr. Price
faces the river. At Little Hell, the currents
still argue, their conflicts enduring longer

than warring theologies and those who wield
them. The Vicar is standing but leans, bruised
by time and loggers who came for the pine.

Feral hogs have gnawed its roots in search
of an easy meal. Still, it grips the sandy soil
as though it fears its next incarnation,

the service to which its parts will be put.
I will not see what happens next,
but I wish it could know I wish it well.

Variations on a Theory

Perhaps parents are like one
theory of the universe—
stalled burst into potential,
then slow collapse into
quivering spark—with this one
difference: tumbling into
itself, the universe will
be unaware.
               Eight decades
have hushed her into murmurs.
Unsure of volume, how to
modulate what she cannot
hear, she hums half-thoughts for fear
of shouting secrets of her
muted world.
               And the man,
who younger draped both ends
of the couch when lying straight,
whose natural gait was another's
trot, slumps in the passenger's
seat, curved like a turtle tipped
on its back, the weight of the world
at last too great.

Philip Belcher

Semi-Private

Anything to relieve the
boredom of Gordon's
carping. In the fluorescent
day of long-term care,
evening and morning are one,
fused by the soldered
groans of two old men.
He once spoke to the night, *This
is my reward for a life lived by rules.*
Jerked from a tired dream of
kindling too wet for fire and
leaning over the bed rail, I
moaned a grudging assent.
Nothing readied us for this
opulent misery.
Prattling on, Gordon conjured
quarrels won, loves lost. Muttered
random names in the dark.
Satisfying but unfair
to think of him as
under delusions more
varied than my own.
We hope only for one day's
Xerox of the last:
yearning is luxury;
zest, a noun best forgotten.

My Groans, My Flies

I feel for my crescent of family
at the bed, offering what they believe
relief by releasing words from their
bulging creels of speech, letting them swim

about the room like rainbows returned
to the stream. They urge me to cast, hook word
after word. The words, though, swirl in a dumb
foam. The children are repulsed by my wet groans,

my flies, confident that the angler's at fault,
that more effort would yield more tugs on the line.
They cannot grasp that I will never
again fill a creel, reel words from the deep

pools of speech but only dream of the catch,
the iridescent syllables. What use
is language in a time of decline? A monster
out of reach, even with a double haul.

Philip Belcher

Talking to Worms

You might fear that this will be
a sentimental lament
about the square of sunlight
falling on my father's lap,
pain docked in his hip, dimming
penlight of recognition,
the chorus of memories
receding in the corner.
But this is not that. It is
instead not much different
from the talk you might have with
your dog, this second person
address, this urging of worms
to return to their chores now
that I've turned them into late
September's tattered light, cut
some with the hoe, buried them
again, several as long
and thick as young snakes, scooped them
aside to make room for the
redbud in the mulched clay by
the retaining wall. I want
them back down there now to do
my bidding, to caress young
roots loosening from the ball
to make their way in the dark.

Down Dog

Before the salted drop splashed
on the wood veneer, before
my forehead filled my palms as
I read the poem about
a boy, a father, and an
old abortion that robbed them
both and two others besides,
before I closed the office
door filled with smoked glass that veils
the ambition of others,
before I arrived first in
the suite and the fluorescents
overhead blinked awake, I
drove the thirteen miles to work
watching fog rise to feather
the peak of Pisgah, wondering
whether we ever grieve a
single loss or always draw
others in: the woman, sick,
bending into a yogi's
pose before the sun draws its
bead on the day; the beagle
I put down Wednesday, her tongue
lolling pink on the mat in
the vet's bereavement room; or
the man who gave me the dog
for safekeeping, gripping the
rails of his walker as he
shuffled away from us both.

Philip Belcher

CNA

To him, through thick weathers of morphine,
headwinds of anesthesia, she was the girl
who came when he pressed the red button
clipped to his sheet. He neither knew her name
nor cared but reached for her as a baby might
stretch toward its mother from the crib.
His wife, vigilant and mute in the corner,
thumbed a catalogue and watched this woman
assume command of the room, preach to her
congregation of one. She nested her shoulder
beneath his, bore his dying weight from bed
to chair, and in one turn choreographed
the toileting of an old man. She gloved
as if the latex were silk and wiped the floor
by his feet. If his anger, rising in those days
like a hail-laden storm, provoked more from her
than a hunch of fate's contempt, she never said.

Wick (Rome 2014)

for my father

A wick in Santa Maria Maggiore
    lists in its wavering flame.

The blue skirt teases the wax
    wet in the round tin.

The yellow blouse shudders in the breeze
    from the open door. Sweet

from the censer's pass, a priest
    stops after mass to gather

along the shelf the few candles
    still lit and sweep the rest

into a half-shut drawer
    to wait for another fire.

January 2015

Each day this month he has rolled
his chair to the window, peered
between red leaves at the sky.
This morning the nurse saw him
bent, his hands moving near his
feet, the pot on its side by
the wheel. He patted the soil
into a mound, tried to plant
the poinsettia in the carpet's
shallow mulch. We are not
surprised. He has always loved
the soil—its smell, its sift
through the sieve of his fingers,
its vow that something else comes.

The Sovereign

After scrolling through the solid woods,
I chose The Sovereign, its underlid
a sunburst of champagne velvet,

and closed the laptop lid.
Built in a Bamberg shop twenty miles
from where it will hold the corpse

and be laid inside a Wilbur Monticello
vault like a nesting box, The Sovereign
stands out from the rest: The Janie,

a busy cedar; the cherry and pompous
Ambassador; the mahogany Remington
and the oak Benson; the McKinsey,

deep poplar. He would be pleased
that it's an understated pecan,
sophisticated in its lack of pretension.

Pecan, like the tree at the parsonage
on Academy Street, the bark for years
flecked with skin from the knees
and arms of the neighborhood's young.

Invoice

Here is the itemized list:

"basic services," whatever those might be: $2570

embalming: $825

optional visitation: $250

ceremony: $325 (price the same, church or graveside, double if both)

transportation of the body: $400–$600 (depending on distance)

other automotive equipment, maybe the contraption that holds the casket and folds as it slides in the hearse—gurney, maybe: $270

ambiguous "Memorial Package": $125

cemetery charges (presumably for the diggers): $1385

casket—Dupree Pecan: $3460 (The Sovereign—same casket, different name)

Wilbur Monticello Vault: $910

and SC Sales Tax (of course): $305 and change

And one more item—unlisted "other preparations."
For $85, John Henry Mole, or maybe his father John,
will wash and disinfect my father, *for the safety
of the funeral home staff, family and friends
and also for dignity and respect of the deceased,*
as if the deceased will be even the slightest bit concerned.

Philip Belcher

Gardener

What peace might come from his portrait
leaning toward my desk from the wall?

The peace of knowing one's lineage:
tribe of wet-eyed lovers of hounds;

farmers who risked livers to spray peach
trees for blight; teetotalers who filled pie pans

with Schlitz to seduce and drown slugs.
And it is here in the study where ink smears

history, where the graft of memory's fiction
thrives on the trunk of what was. Here is the son:

damaged limb scabbing, prepared to fork and bloom
in a show still governed by the root.

Acoustics

How does Barnwell sound from inside the ground?
I ask this way because I know you cannot see

or, if you can, not beyond the quilted silk
of the lid. Or, if that has somehow fallen in

after only four years, not beyond the vault
that levels the gravesite to suit the dog walkers

or the high schoolers fucking on their blankets.
And while I'm wondering, have the sutures that closed

your lips snapped, or loosened even a little, to let your mouth
drop open as it did when you dozed, warm beneath the *Times*,

for twenty minutes after lunch? Asleep, you always looked
        amazed.
Can you hear the slosh of traffic where Jackson Street dumps

its light sediment of cars and trucks into the four-lanes' marsh?
What about the constant thump of basketballs on the court

that covers what used to be the public pool,
the one we left when black families came?

Can you hear bass rising at the hatchery beside Jones Creek,
the spillway at the dam where water once slapped the wheel?

Philip Belcher

Or scuttlebutt at the two-pump Exxon that Johnny ran until
Lou Gehrig's grabbed him from behind, the grumbles from the
    card game

in the room behind the bait shop where your deacons plied
    our beagle with beer?
Mostly, I hope it's quiet for you—maybe the sounds of the moles'

small industry in the earth outside, rumbles of thunder,
subtle shifts of soil and rock: a posthumous gardening.

You, finally the introvert, swallowed by the black dirt you loved.

II
SOMETHING BORROWED

Aging is growth of a new but a very fine hearing that only to silence hearkens.

—Joseph Brodsky, "1972"

Another Good Morning

Across the room, the dog's chest swells and sinks
like the Mediterranean on a blue and windless day.

Her snoring hums both alto and bass, and the thin
snare rolling beneath suggests a rest that's ocean deep.

The rain drums a soft stroll on the roof, and I sit alone
with the dog, wrapped in a sea-green fleece, reading

Pavese and watching January's choir of sparrows gather
in the drizzle to assail a meddling hawk. Their early

industry does not embarrass me into action or coax
more than a stretch in the rocking chair. I'm hiking

with Pavese above Santo Stefano Belbo, and the wind
in the grapes sounds like the breath of a sleeping hound.

Philip Belcher

Donnie with Baby and Cows 1999
after the photograph by Shelby Lee Adams

With a pat on the side of the plastic bin,
Donnie called from the hill two cows
and a yearling bull. The bull wandered off

to the boy standing beneath the oak, but the cows
crowded Donnie under the bowl of the TV dish
he'd nailed to the mountain with three

steel poles. After a minute under the lamp
on my desk, one Guernsey begins to glow,
and her eyes, like the eyes of all penned

beasts, succeed in their plea for attention.
I imagine Adams unscrewing the lens,
sliding the tripod's legs into their sleeve,

and loading his truck for the next shot
by a Malibu raised on blocks, a chicken
dusting by. I think of Donnie, the baby

held close, the boy and the bull, all walking toward
the barn's dark yawn, the dull plink of bells
as the cows climb the hill. I almost miss

that Donnie's tucked his blue-jean cuffs
behind the tongues of his Faded Glory
boots and wonder whether Adams staged

GENTLE SLAUGHTER

that touch, aimed light at Donnie's feet,
whether poverty and pride can be joined
anymore without a subtle prop.

Philip Belcher

Eric with Spike the Rooster 2001

after the photograph by Shelby Lee Adams

There is no ease between this boy,
this bird, no languid pose behind
the house peeling its way to soil.
Waiting for the sun to strut
from the coop-gray cloud and feather
the afternoon with heat, for shadows
to arc beneath the nails fastening paint
to the baked oak planks, Eric clasps
the rooster to his waist with the crook
of his arm, holds his antagonist close.
Its wattle and comb bloom dark
on the thick white stem of its neck.
From the feet, talons jut like blades.
Eric clamps the hocks with one hand,
with the other slants the shanks away
from his thigh. He knows Spike's
abiding rage, knows the hostage,
bitter and wild, will rake its spurs
across his groin unless its legs
are bound or unless it is freed.

Bird in Hand

after Shelby Lee Adams' photograph Anne with Pigeon, '95

Of all the photographs of people
with beasts—*Enos Holding Snapping
Turtles, '07, Jane with Diddles, '94,*

Shithead the Pony and the Noble Family,
'03—this print of Anne cupping a pigeon
bites like an ax into pine's soft meat.

This woman has become a tree. Skin as etched
as bark, her face the whorl of a severed
limb scored into silence by the mountain's

taloned weather. In the foreground, the dark
bird stares from the nest of Anne's fingers.
It's as if she wants me to take her prize,

to see what she sees behind
the pigeon's eye, to share the panic
felt through the feathered chest.

Philip Belcher

Frame of Reference

> *after Diane Arbus's photograph* Child with Toy Hand Grenade in Central Park, N.Y.C. 1962

Some memories click into place
like a .38's hammer being cocked.
I remember the park on a day unable
to twist itself toward cold or warmth.

My nephew, Carl, pretty as any girl
when his legs were clean and his hair
was straight, stood lock-kneed at a bend
in the path. He mugged for the lady,

wincing as if slapped each time
the shutter tripped and the bulb
flashed. Even from behind, I knew
the cast of his face, the grimace he wore

for photographs mailed to his father
in the wet mirage of Saigon. Carl's
right hand gripped the play grenade
I'd buried along with eggs and toys

in Easter grass. His other, a pale
and empty claw, tipped the scale
of him leftward, as if absence
weighed more than I could know.

After Hours With *The Iliad*

When he hears the paper slap the porch,
    he stands from the chair from which he's fought
alongside both long-haired Achaeans
    and stallion-loving Trojans, aroused
by the white-armed Andromache, Helen
    with her scented breasts, and walks
into the ambush of fog hushed
    on the ridge outside.

At times like this he pretends
    he is Hector or one of the Ajaxes flanked
in battle by war-starved comrades,
    wielding a lance looted from a rival, sporting
a helmet crested with horsehair
    bent in the wind, defended from the waxing
assault by a shield of seven
    nested hides ringed with bronze.

But this morning the porch light slings
    his shadow against the fog,
and he confronts not an image somehow
    subordinate, lying at his feet
like a Thracian whose breastplate
    he might haul back to the long curved
ship, but by his equal—
    or his master: larger than his middle-aged frame,

the wet drops of its face a floating
    blank mass, the body's bulk not fixed but part

of the illuminated bank of white,
> matching his moves limb for limb. A shiver,
and he retreats inside to cast his lot with the Argives. But choosing
> to side with the victor does not subdue
his fear. And Achilles, still raging over
> Agamemnon's theft of Briseis,
the king's strut as he dragged her over
> the wave-packed sand and back
to his ships, remains aloof, urging
> Patroclus into the fray.

Fear of Giants

after Diane Arbus's photograph A Jewish Giant at Home with His Parents in the Bronx, N.Y. 1970

Rabbi Mueller stopped calling him Samson
when my son at ten looked down on me.
By twelve, he'd torn the tightening collar

of school, and I saw his future frown.
Last week, Bart's Deli named him worker
of the month. He stocks the highest shelves.

Now we wait, our evening service, as he steps
in from the job, conquers the door with his cane,
his limp. My wife's hands nest on the ledge

of her hips, her mouth's delighted o telling
him, telling me, of her triumph, that this Titan
began in her. I look straight at his waist,

hands moling my pockets for dark. Myths
have come and gone since I brushed his hair
while he stood. Tonight, I sit by his brow,

surveying the baffling terrain of his face,
and muster a waning affection.

Philip Belcher

Kentucky Conclave

after Shelby Lee Adams' photograph Eric 2001

Christopher Hitchens, the dying atheist,
seems to be winning. Irenaeus, his robe

damp in the fog, twists his beard into
a rope and confers with Jesus.

Jürgen Moltmann, rumpled from his trans-
Atlantic flight, folds his hands like a church

and presses the steeple to his lips. All four
shift to look at Eric on the warped porch step,

nine years old and staring over their heads
into the dark. Popping a wheelie on Eric's

shirt, Scooby Doo spreads his arms,
lets cartoon wind commandeer his tongue.

A cheap print of Christ framed in rain-fouled
pine is fixed to the wall behind Eric's head:

suffering nailed to fading clapboard. Alone
with Scooby and Christ, Eric hears a murmur

near the Ford. Irenaeus insists the boy may
choose to dodge misery's quick lunge. Moltmann

rebuts with his knowledge of evil—the Belgian
forests, his time in the camps. Jesus is miffed

that no one has yet arrived to save the boy.
But Hitchens, bald and sick, finds a stick

and scratches *Scooby* in the dirt. Scooby,
ridiculous and wild, the only one still free.

Philip Belcher

Some Local Cindy

    after Billy Collins' "The Rival Poet"

You daydreamed of trading places
and lives with the rival poet posing
on the marble staircase, his arm
graced by the *Contessa Maria Teresa
Isabella Veronica Multalire Eleganza
Bella Ferrari.* And now you are there
and have been standing for a while—
so long, in fact, it seems you've
become part of the statuary in the corner
of the landing by the potted bonsai laurel.
You should know that the Cindys do not
miss you. They're quite aware you'd swap
the lot of them for the Contessa, prefer
Beethoven to Bocephus, Barbaresco
to Bud. But, just so you know, mine
is not any old local Cindy but Cindy Birt—
yes, that Cindy—who read every word
on every page of every assignment
in Mrs. Keel's literature class, even
Silas Marner, who between classes
blew through the Brontës' bleak
topographies and tiptoed through
the back alleys of Dickens, who clenched
a flashlight between her teeth to read
in a tent of covers in her pink room
near Williston, who preferred books
to boys, books to grades, books to
everything but her dream of working

at the reference desk of the Biblioteca
Medicea-Laurenziana, emerging
at the end of her shift into Florentine sun,
and walking home, a book in one hand
and, in the other, the arm of a minor
Tuscan poet who looks at no one but her.

Philip Belcher

Memoir

> *after Diane Arbus's photograph* Tattooed Man at a Carnival, Md. 1970

After a darkroom hour,
    I knew a second shoot
        would be a waste. The focus

would never be Jim's skin
    but the irises leaking his dreams
        into twilight's monochrome.

Pinning prints to the drying
    line, I reread the aborted memoir
        etched on his body's thinning film.

Across his brow, a skull
    bit a cigarette. Helixed smoke
        bothered an errant star, while an entire

constellation cowered beneath his neck
    in a cavern rimmed by tendons
        defending his throat. The python

cinching his waist squeezed
    words up until they spilled
        from Jim's eyes as light, telling a story

he would never articulate.

Aviary

    after Tim Barnwell's photograph Emma Mills on Porch with Chickens, 1982

I don't much care what they'll think,
folks who'll see this photograph
hung in Tim's shop window, what
they'll assume about my life
in Dry Branch. When they see
the hollows in my face, thin ropes
of my arms, they'll see a type,
I guess, woman bent against
mountain with few means to leave.
But I am here of my own accord,
free as these chickens scuffling
for split corn spilled on the porch.
They are not caged or clipped
but hop and hitch there by
the Sealtest crate, small gleaners
oblivious to their fate.

III
BOY ON FIRE

... Filling with light,

Each leaf feels its way out,
Each a mad bible of patience.

—Larry Levis, "The Crimes of the Shade Trees"

Luminary

I saw them first in Old Salem, candles
rooted in sand anchoring white bakery

bags, both sides of residential streets
lined like airstrips one month a year,

a faint lane to sixteenth-century Spain
where bonfires lit roadways and churchyards

during Las Posadas to honor the search
by Mary and Joseph for a room.

And now they line the sides of Franklin Street
in Barnwell beginning mid-December,

and I remember other flames
along this curb, the gutter tongued with fire

on autumn Saturdays when children swarmed
the lawn and raked leaves toward the street,

when Brenda Paulk, Penny Still, and Letcher
Correll, ten years before he, his wife, and baby girl

died by blade and flame, advanced
the skirmish line of oak and pecan leaves

across our acre lot, each armed with a steel-
tined rake, blisters gloving their palms.

The fathers, benevolent foremen, paced
the sidewalk, gauging the wind as if they

could predict its sudden shifts with a wet
finger aimed at the sky, banking leaves

and eyeing with casual distrust the sizzling
skeletons ghosting up in new thermals,

little kites of fire drifting out of reach.
They doused the rare fugitive

that refused to die on its own.
When I was eight, the age of maturity

for leaf burning, my father
handed me the box of Safety Strikes

and watched me light the leaves along the line,
a crackling bracelet with five orange charms.

The fires spread until they joined and raised
a curtain of smoke that veiled the church across

the way and conjured tears that rutted trails
in the dirt fields of our cheeks. Woody Bennicker said

that from his Cessna Saturdays looked
as if the whole town were burning,

Gentle Slaughter

smoke rising from the streets, orderly
until smeared by wind above the trees.

I remember such a Saturday when the breeze
sheared back toward the house, and a cinder

buried its head in Letcher's polyester shirt.
He ran toward home, screaming for his mother,

watching the bud of flame bloom on his chest
and melt breast pocket to skin.

And then he obeyed the formula—stopped,
dropped, and rolled on the grass. I remember,

as Letcher ran past, my baby sister watching
from the screen porch, pointing, then remarking,

Boy on fire.

Philip Belcher

I Spent Most of Elementary School Fearing Quicksand

The few other means of death I dreamed
were wrapped in glory's sinew: leaping
in front of the six o'clock freight to untie
Pam Creech from the track; shoving my

cousin off the road before the red Camaro
hit; throwing my chest on a hand grenade
to protect my men on Omaha Beach.
But no narrative redeemed my luckless fall

into the saucer of sopping earth that looked
like Sunday's oatmeal bowl, my topmost
hairs pausing a second, as if I'd found
the bottom, before slipping under without

rippling the surface. Worst of all was the limb
lying a hand out of reach and the Braves cap
floating to show my mother why I'd not come
home. Gilligan always found a patch on his island

and saved Mary Ann and the Skipper with vines
or a rope from the wreck. In 1974, Mel Brooks
made it a joke in *Blazing Saddles*. Bart and his
partner pumped a handcar to the end of the line

and into a quicksand sump. The deputy lassoed
the cart and left the two black men to balance

their way on a sunken rail to drier ground.
By then I knew I'd never seen the stuff

and probably never would. Television quicksand
disappeared toward the end of Vietnam, as Cronkite
read the news of MIAs and monsoons and parents
grew tired of children pretending to drown.

Philip Belcher

Elsewhere

She loathes television's depiction of women
as *gun-toters with breasts hanging out over
their necklines and skirts up to their elsewheres.*

Eighty-seven and, as she writes to *The Herald*,
one foot in the grave and the other on ice,
Mrs. Chattie Songer Hart longs for a bureau

of mothers empowered to scour the screen
clean of human skin and other vulgarities.
I can imagine her horrified by Reality TV

or by Angelina Jolie, the bulging lips, the vial
of Billy Bob's blood hung between her breasts.
But let's not throw the baby out with the bathwater,

for the unintended consequence of piety is often
the most severe. Had Mrs. Hart's desire been
fulfilled a generation back, American boys

would have missed the principal joy
of the Winter Olympics. I have not forgotten
yearnings conjured in black and white,

Peggy Fleming kissing gold in Grenoble
the year figure skating trounced baseball
as Barnwell's favorite pastime, when the double

Gentle Slaughter

axel shoved the grand slam into a hall locker
and left it there for the games' duration.
As we lay on the rug in '68, chins cupped

in our palms and watching Peggy skate,
her arms reaching toward the camera,
toward us, our limits seemed to recede.

Our imaginations leapt as she leapt.
We felt the honed blade of desire
and began to imagine elsewhere.

Philip Belcher

Missing a Wound

Dr. Colquitt spent most of his days
with Barnwell County's mares and cows,

reaching in them shoulder-deep to ease
a breach, maneuver the legs and head.

He made time for an occasional pet
but refused to touch ferrets or Phil Prater's

snakes. He did tend my beagle after her war
with the cur that skulked under the Catholic

church, pried apart the bloody lips
of the furrow ripped through the dog's

flank, and filled the cleft with a white
powder he seemed to use for everything.

Home, she stepped from floorboard
to gravel, limped toward her spot by

the boxwood hedge, but stopped and curled
in the grass. A white worm inched

from a fold just below the neck. I spread
the fur with my thumbs and found a wound

that Colquitt missed—a pit the size
of a walnut, pulsing with maggots,

heads buried deep, feasting on the part
of her that did not wait to die.

Philip Belcher

Slur

Ten years have scrubbed most of the fire
from the cinder blocks. The lawn has ceded
its grass to sand, to bottles tossed from cars
on Highway 3. Until today, I've never stopped,

listened to the wind blow through the soybeans
and the ribs of the double-wide. That night
comes back, and I hear the band at the armory
covering Skynyrd's "Simple Man."

I see in shards of glass the sneer of Tanner Bates
drunk on Chivas and lust, stumbling into
Andrew's wife, cupping her breast too long,
Andrew reddening until *faggot* breaks

through the bars of his teeth. And Tanner,
following them home, waiting in his Ford
until the sitter's gone and all the lights are out.
No sound but the pines' soft sweep, like a sheet

sliding over skin. This man, a friend until
three hours ago, lifts a five-gallon can
from the trunk, empties it in one turn
around the trailer, and waits for flames

to tear the dark. I remember the preacher—
tall behind three caskets, singing "His Eye
Is on the Sparrow" louder than anyone else,
and remarking how these parents read

the Bible to their daughter every night,
how when dawn stabbed the smoking lot
and the firemen twisted their hoses closed
a page of Leviticus washed to the street.

Philip Belcher

The Lesson

On a bench cut from the stump of a willow oak,
I sat in the dark, impatient for the promised lesson.

The transformer hummed a gray alto
into the pines, moths hurled themselves into

the carport light, and Gail opened the double-
glass door to her father's house. Wrapped

in Jay Wilson's football jacket, she came
to me across the grass, an olive moon of hip

waxing through her jeans' ripped seam.
Her smile explained all I would ever need

to know about pity and power, and I raised
my lips as if to sip the stars. For five dry

seconds, our mouths contended, the pressure
heavier than friendship, hers lighter than lust,

a contest too brief, too calm, her hand channeling
the agony of all young manhood into my thigh.

Question for Heavy

If I could find Heavy, persuade him
to lower the theodolite

from his shoulder and lean his elevation
rod against the pine,

I would ask whether the red hourglass
splashed onto the widow's

black abdomen marked for him, as it did
for me, a gift, an intrusion

of the primary into the rote of June.
I would ask

what moved him, after another day of figuring
earth's angles, to shine

his flashlight between the bars of the grate
draining 1978's rain

from southbound 21, to stick his thumb
into the dark and pluck

the chaotic silk like a banjo string until
she rolled and graced us all.

Philip Belcher

Prelude to a Hunt

In the bed of the sky-blue Ford,
two crates quivered with the consternation
of caged hounds, rose tips of noses

poking through rusted mesh like knuckles
of the newly jailed. We drove the roads
near Kline—asphalt, gravel, rutted dirt—

and parked near the tail of a snake of trucks.
The dogs whined while we peeled a turtle
from the front left tire. Following cairns

of spent tobacco, Harvey Birt led me
to a clearing ringed with Styrofoam
spittoons and throbbing with bearded men

frying fish and oiling guns.
I thought of the disc of salmon
on my brother's supper plate, the single

square of butter clinging to a mound
of grits. At 6:00, he would bike to church
for Sword Drill, find Zechariah 1

on command, the object speed, not truth;
destination, not journey. I preferred
these men who thrived behind the bars

GENTLE SLAUGHTER

of their expectations, spitting out bones,
tossing scraps to their dogs, savoring
the stew that would fuel their night's pursuit.

Philip Belcher

Otherwise Gentle

Every opening day, before our first shots
broke November's truce, he stopped
by the gate on the way to the field,
lit a menthol True, and blew a ring
in tribute to his old pointer, Jack—
Jack, who gummed dead birds into
the pocket of his camouflaged vest,
who never once bruised the sweet
white meat, never required a lesson
from the tip of a sweetgum sprig.
Now, Easter in Barnwell, sun glinting
like a barrel through the oak's cocked
green, fields ripe with patio homes,
all the quail scuttling under hedgerows
ten miles away in Kline, and I remember
Harold Geddings hurdling broom straw
bent with ice, his bellowed *whoa* ricocheting
off poplars lining the irrigation ditch,
one fist gripping a Browning Light Twenty,
the other hoisting a chain to sling
at an English Setter born too fond
of sparrows and mice. Harold, veteran
lathe-minder and lecturer on the South's
finer arts: how to breathe at the nucleus
of a covey's blast, how to drop a dove
by aiming ahead into nothing,
how to honor days clear enough to spot
not only the grackle crouching in straw
but the fly it snaps from the air.

The Cards

Why do old men shoot themselves
in early spring? Perhaps dust
motes riding bars of April
sun to the woolen mill's floor
remind the tired of options
faced just once then lost. Now May
brings word that Jake, long truant
from the looms, molded his back
to the bathtub's bend, gripped
the stock with his feet and ensured
another empty seat when
the weave-room alumni meet
on Monday for coffee and hearts,
sure, as always, that one
of the regulars will cheat.

Undressing the Dead

Chaplain's apprentice in blazer and tie,
he knew little of God and less of death

but helped the orderlies wrest from the hearse
a body three days into its June swell.

He pushed the gurney to the morgue, stayed
to help the nurse wash the corpse.

She loaned him a pair of scissors, rehearsed
by snipping the air's loose weave. Gloved,

they cut his shirt, unfastened the belt halving
his frame. Liquid smells flanked their masks.

They each slit a pant leg starting at the cuff,
pulled the cloth back as if peeling bruised fruit.

In the morgue's enduring winter, they worked
the blades an inch at a time, aiming away

from the swollen sex, dark heart ready
to burst, hung from a brittle stem.

Renaissance Man

for Albert Blackwell

Only once in thirty years have we spoken,
but reading Epictetus reminded me of you:
biking to campus on your 10-speed Schwinn,
the daily khakis and the button-down, blue,
the volume of Stoics in your messenger bag.
In my study, your Schleiermacher monograph
leans against *The Selected Letters* of Keats.
A pipe cleaner marks the title page, the kindness
you inscribed there. And the modest light
on my books brings back the permanent dusk
of your room in Furman Hall where once
I found you sitting cross-legged on your desk,
humming a Morley madrigal and puzzling
your way through Dürer's *Melencolia I*.

Philip Belcher

It's Pronounced [tree-u*h* n]

I love the Antiques Road Show—how its treasures
confound or confirm my intuition, how smart
the latter makes me feel, how it flays
my idea of worth. The rickety old rocker,
$10,000; the Tiffany lamp a fake.
And in Savannah, how the empty wooden box
the size of a card deck—chipped mosaic
on its lid (I'd have tossed it in the fire, fed
it to the stove)—turns out to be Tunbridge ware
(as if I know what that means) and valued
by the twin appraisers at enough to pay my mortgage
for a year. It doesn't even yield the needles
and thread it was meant to bear, its purpose
irrelevant, its maker's intent dismissed.

Lines on the Installation of My Brother
    Cullowhee, March 29, 2012

Do you remember Millett, the sand castle
we built at the edge of the woods, the tunnels
we drilled with twigs from the pine, the hickory
nuts we bowled through that new light?

And Little Hell, that bend in the Savannah
where currents annoyed the dull water
by the bank, pleated the pools like folds
in a purple robe, where we picked among

cypress knees for clams, pried them to death
with our thumbs? Can you hear our father
in the headwater of his channeled life,
telling us as he looked across the river

at Georgia about our great-uncle James,
the one who drowned in a whirlpool
(or maybe he was the one who put a pistol
in his mouth), pointing at eddies and the holes

they sucked in the water, calling our mother
to come close to the edge, she who was never
easy near water? Can you see the procession
of little nobles in our back yard: the Corrells,

the Queens, the two lovely Paulks?
I do not know why these images rear up now,

Philip Belcher

stampede their solemn riders into this warm
Appalachian night as I plan the trip to Cullowhee,

where the Tuckasegee licks the edge of your
campus, where freshmen swim and paddle
near shoals their parents would tell them to shun.
I cannot help but think of you now as regal:

Susan, as queen; your winter view
of the mountain looming over
the Chancellor's house, a window onto your
kingdom after the maples surrender their fire.

When I think of you now I see only gold.
You have assumed the mantel of power
that slipped from our father's slumped
shoulders. You have climbed to a height

you once imagined and in your dreams
summited, and you, like I, want only to look
ahead. But on evenings when you walk toward
home and consider in the stubborn light

the students in your care, remember those
Saturdays at Little Hell, how we skipped
bits of quartz across the flow,
taught chipped stones to fly.

Dead of Winter

We hardly notice the sky on our walk
from porch door to car, carrying small
packages and leftover cheese from the last
family Christmas with my brother.
We know he will be dead this time next year
and are wrapped tight as buds in that thought
on our several trips to burden our trunks
with boxes and bags, ignoring torn ribbons
flailing in the wind. The cold stiffens
our impulse to look down, to steel ourselves
against seeing what still thrives: the sundog
peering from the western sky; the laced
geometry of veins lining the few unraked leaves
that died in October; crystals rimming
the koi pond; and the orange blaze
of fish, patient beneath the ice.
Perhaps such beauty is no match for our present
sorrow. Perhaps no beauties are.
So we stare at our feet, hearing only
their shuffle through frozen remnants
of green, the dirty rags of snow.

IV
GENTLE SLAUGHTER

*To live in hearts we leave behind
is not to die.*

—Claudia Emerson, "Curing Time"

Ode to the God of Dogs

after Hayden Carruth

Six in the morning, the sun uncertain of its rise,
this hound lying by my chair, her eyes and forehead

lifting at my every shift. I yearn to say the words
"ontological" and "existential," the latter for the way

it fills the mouth with sibilant grit, the former for the Os
it spins on my tongue. Something essential is up and about.

And praise, that infrequent guest, raps her warm paw
on the back porch door, wags her way into the light.

Whether you exist is a question I choose not to ask today.
Nor will I button my well-worn sweater of doubt.

These winter days I sense you in the barren fields,
in the unnamable grey of the coon hound's flank,

the beagle's unnerving bay, the bloodhound's determined lunge
at the end of the sheriff's leash. The grand chorus of howls

at dawn fades like mercy and settles the house. O god
of the hound, the Brittany, the chocolate Lab,

god of the pointer, the setter, and breeds less enamored
of death, if others live in your pack, implore them to lean

from their jealous table and look down on one man
aiming not for a place in their pantheon but content

in his woods by a Herald stove, reddening in the heat
from his last block of beech, a bluetick's chin on his boot.

Lines Composed in the Jim Barkley Toyota Service Department Lounge

> *Without the aid of prejudice and custom, I should not be able to find my way across the room.*
> —William Hazlitt

That he smells like lilacs is the great surprise,
this man in overalls complaining of gout—
the reason he needs the clerk's help to find
the Tacoma's VIN. But lilac is clear.

Had all but olfactory sense been bound,
gagged and stuffed in a trunk, I would think
a breeze had trailed a teenaged girl through
the sliding glass door or that a woman

my mother's age had shuffled to the seat
backing mine to wait for the buzzer's signal that her
Camry was sporting new tires. But it is a man,
a farmer by the looks of him, not long out

of the beans. Beyond him the lounge spreads
like a surgery waiting room: coffee, pretzels
racked on the wall, camera balls in the ceiling tiles.
Here, the children have their own room.

They slide plastic blocks along red wires
spiraling up from an eight-by-six wooden base,
a roller coaster diminished and slow. They've
finished their game of hangman on the board,

Philip Belcher

insulated by fortified glass from the teenager
professing his love for the yellow Camaro
in the Gently Used lot, that vast plain of temptation.
Prying a slab of caramel from his molars, he swears

he'll find a way to pay: "Goddammit, Ma, I will!"
But I'm struck still by the man and his April scent—
that and the segregation of the children,
the cartoons on their big-screen TV presumed

more suitable than the weight-loss infomercial
spilling a buxom starlet into the lounge's expanse
and every man peeping over the edge of his
Car and Driver to glimpse the blonde

promising results *and more* in just two weeks.
How different this is than standing by the icebox
outside the service bay of Johnny Bessinger's Esso
in 1971. Harold smoking his fifth True Blue

of a young Saturday, Harvey stuffing Red Man
into his cheek while stretching the truth about
how many possums he'd shot at the dump,
Murray raising the ante by comparing

the new secretary at the zipper plant to Catherine
Deneuve, and Johnny listening to it all from under
the car, unscrewing the filter and draining burnt
oil into the pan—the warm rush, slow drip—

Gentle Slaughter

two years before Lou Gehrig's cocooned him in its tight suit.
The smell was oil and grease, and talk was of the new
lathe at the bomb plant, the way the Geiger counters
seldom ticked since March's steam release, the cracked

valve. This, after all, was how boys then learned to be men—
osmosis and time. The segregations were simple, inherited.
Lilacs belonged in gardens or wafting from Murray's wife
as she led the Pledge and the school day's opening prayer.

But Johnny's gone. Murray and Harvey, too. Harold
watches shadows crawl close to his chair, dust mount
the Browning racked above the mantel, and all
distinctions that once organized life blur, this life

with fewer lines and uncertainty about who drew them,
boys who curse their mothers and mothers who take it,
children behind glass, men unafraid to smell like flowers,
as if it were the most natural thing in the world.

Philip Belcher

Dry

There are worse things than leaving
with an empty creel: being
deaf to the river's bright scales,
ignoring the dignity
of trout, spurning elegance
in thrall to success and speed.
So, I pity the nymph's rough
body, the unkempt thorax
dubbed from a cottontail's flank.
Call me a purist, but I'd
rather wait in vain for a trout
to sip from the thin skin
of the Davidson an Elk
Hair Caddis, an Adams Midge,
or a Pale Evening Dun than
tie a nymph and pinch a split-
shot weight to the line. Morning's
storm clouded the stream with silt,
but a Gray Ghost bucktail two
feet down would seduce the Brown
from her gravel bed. I could
catch dinner with a Black-Nosed
Dace or a Tellico but
would rather watch the Blue-Winged
Parachute ski the eddy
massaging this granite slab.

Bait

As if reading roots by Braille, both boys
finger the bank below the surface, feeling
for shafts where giant catfish, snug in their
cool gray suits, lurk for food. Each finds

a hole, sucks in a breath and sticks in his
naked arm pit-deep, hoping for jaws and not
the shears of a snapper's beak. The blond one
yells, yanks a thirty-pounder to the sand,

but trips over a rotting carp. The catfish loosens
its mouth and splashes back into the Edisto,
as if spitting the boy up on land. Whether
it's noise or silt or both, no more bites today.

An empty stringer for their father. They piss
in the woods and glare across the river at my
8-foot rod, the spinning rig and gray Bean
vest, the tub full of livers for bait. No doubt

they hear my fish thrashing in ice. The boys
untie their boat from a cypress knee and jerk
the motor to life. Before they round the bend,
they slow and shoot two turtles off a log.

Beatitude

> *Blessed are the meek, for they shall inherit the earth.*
> —Matthew 5:5

Beneath the dawn redwood's broadening
green yawn thrives a row of seven azaleas,
their canopies bridged by bumble bees ferrying

pollen from anther to pistil and back. The bees
do not aspire to live in the middle air of cardinals
or the hawk-scoured wind above the trees.

They do not aspire at all but rather excavate
their sticky cave in the crepe myrtle's shade,
unconcerned with the size or fate of other nests

or hives. In June, I saw an eagle drop a headless bass
on a spit of sand fingering the Wateree and join
her mate in a sycamore crest, her shadow hushing all

the small mammals on the bank. The harbinger
passed. The beaver resumed battling the current,
and the rat cooled in the cypress roots weaving

to reach water, neither mesmerized by what it
could not be, each content to live as if called.

In Tübingen

Jürgen Moltmann smokes alone.
After strolling the Neckar's bank,
he retires to his rooms, writes
all night of his crucified
God. Theology tomes rise
like stones across the plain
of his desk, excuse divine
inaction by positing a present
absence, an absent presence,
as if we should feel pity for God.
Even Moltmann lies awake
at night, fingering a cross
he cannot see and organizing
a defense to Ivan Karamazov's
rebuke, the Russian's contempt
for saviors who offer heavens
built on the cries of a boy
locked up for hurling a stone
at the general's hound and freed
to flee the dogs until they
tear him apart as the mother
looks on. Such are the ends
of absent gods. Fifty now,
I know better what Moltmann
has tried to say. Nothingness
can be palpable, a thing
known only in its passing:
the wind torn by Hölderlin's
Tower, the last hint of cello

Philip Belcher

rising from the hall, the dimple
where the dog lay before
she heard the morning's first
birdsong and nosed her way
into the stubborn dark.

Inquisition

When doves punctuate the power lines
organizing the air above the garden,
they never look away. The cardinal

in the holly twitches toward every compass
point, alert for tragedy or betrayal: squirrels,
the dull yellow cat slinking by, the dog

pawing for fallen eggs beside the ivied
wall, the thieving jay. But the doves,
fat gray hearts, sit and pump

their accusatory coos directly at me,
as if I know what makes them grieve,
as if, somehow, I am responsible.

Philip Belcher

Requiem

At the end of the tractor path
rubbing the edge of the field,

Mr. Haydy waits in his blue Ford.
The hedgerow hides his car

from State Road 9 as the sun
slides below the South's green belt.

He slicks his hair with a dab
of spit. As if he'd lit a fire,

the cab glows from the visor light.
Quarter past eight, the beans lean

away from August's moist breath.
Billy should have been here by now,

wearing the Panthers cap and shorts
he'd worn biking home from school.

He'd been formal on the phone,
as if afraid another was listening.

Haydy beats time to Verdi's *Requiem*
on the steering wheel's leather sheath,

dials the volume up. Wrapped
in the *Sanctus*, lost in his daydream

GENTLE SLAUGHTER

of Billy's steaming back, he fans five
snapshots like a hand of cards.

The sun's last wink blinds
Haydy to the man stepping from

the pines, and the wind muffles
the snap of a chambered slug.

Philip Belcher

Preserved

Where have all the taxidermists gone?
Their mounted skunks and weasels skulk
through the maze of wills and estates

recorded by Dolores Kilner, Charleston
County Registrar of Deeds. Deer busts,
antlered and thick-necked, charge from

mahogany panels in King Street's private
libraries as if the shoulders might yet follow.
Their favorite seemed to be the red fox,

fixed mid-trot on a block of pine, sometimes
mouthing a flopping mink. Bobcats, long
truant from the cypress swamps distilling

the Edisto, ran a close second. They prowl
the shelves of the antique store by the Market.
In 1974, Miss Kilner paid Jack Tolbert,

back from Cambodia and broke, a hundred
dollars to stuff her German Shorthair, Sam,
and set him pointing a covey of porcelain

quail from the sideboard abutting her living
room couch where she watched *The Price
is Right* with Sam for the next thirty years.

Gentle Slaughter

Where have they all gone, these curators
of the rural South? Lots of them are Scots,
so maybe they've gone back home. Some

must moonlight as brewers. Last week, NBC
advertised the "strangest beer in the world,"
The End of History, made in Aberdeenshire.

Bottles are stuffed in road-kill squirrels.
Liquor pours from glass necks jutting
through the mouths' enduring surprise.

Philip Belcher

Blue

The vases, bottles, bowls and plates tucked
into every nook, keeping watch in their mute
symmetry, holding candles erect, lounging
against their pewter scaffolds on the shelf.
The sky, some days, when the fog loosens
its grip on the ridge. The tint of her blouse
in the photograph she gave him. The eyes
above her porcelain cheeks. And his mother's
quilt, spread on the grass at Tanglewood.
I see them recline thirty years ago in June's
wet heat, ignoring the duck as it marches by
still dripping from the pond, and I hear them
ponder changeling clouds tumbling through the sky.
First I hear his question, then her soft reply.

To Dr. Paulson on the Eve of Surgery

For a few hours starting at 6 a.m.,
I will break my vow. You should have
and hold my wife as if she were your own.

Instead of asking her to count back
from ninety-nine, let her hum herself
into anesthesia's yellow maze.

Suggest an old movie tune; she will know it.
The more obscure, the better.
Fill the O.R. with Sinatra. She won't mind.

Arrange the bloom of lights to terrify
the shadows conspiring to darken
your eyes, and rinse her free of every germ

spoiling to mar your work.
Through the length of your body, feel
a stiff tug as you pull the scalpel

through her skin. See lying before you
your own beloved, cold in that room's bright
and sterile winter. When you cut my wife,

avoid the light that breaks from the wounds.
Her pain can blind. Cradle her breasts. Cup
them, as I would, before you lift them off.

Philip Belcher

Reconstruction Sonnet

Our daughter called them tit-tats,
and all of us laughed at her dip
into humor's deep well,
at resorting to ink to restore
the look of being able to feel.
Beneath the slick pink,
squint-eyed scars still score
the fresh, embedded tint.

I am surprised to think *nipple*
when I pry an almond chip
from the ice cream with my lips.
My wife sees me tongue the nut,
nibble the rim of the sugar cone.
Says nothing, then turns. A groan.

New Year, White County, Arkansas

Air vent streamers wag like tongues from the wall
of the Ozark cave. Cold stiffens the stream splitting

the floor, and the cracking ice pops. Beneath the glaze,
blind fish swim, pale sloops defying the current's mute

push. Outside, miles east, peonies bloom green and gold
into the dark. Stars split and fade from flowering

crossettes, and the trailing booms stun three thousand
red-winged blackbirds from the sky. Sunrise sparks,

and the sleepy folk of Beebe wake with a fleeting sense
of the new. Their lawns gleam black and red, as if a slave ship

had wrecked on an inland tide and spilled its bleeding load.

Qilin

Except for the obvious, it looks nothing
like a unicorn, and even the horn curves
gently back, its tip a gradual rose.

The cat ears distract. Yellow eyes
bulge from a lion face. The purple-
striped band unfurls from throat to groin.

The tail, beginning pale as the goatee,
darkens to brown near the end. Torso
more deer than horse, hooves pawing

the website's white space. The unicorn,
by comparison, is dour—twisted horn
photo-shopped fluorescent yellow

onto the brow of a mule standing over
a caption in which even the comma
scoffs: *North Korea Has Found*

a Secret Unicorn Lair, Apparently.
Yes, the Korean Central News Agency
also told a starving people that the hills

cried and birds cooed laments upon
the death of Kim Jong-il. And, yes,
the PRK is an easy target for scorn.

Gentle Slaughter

But you must admire the audacity.
And imagine our delight if they were not,
this once, disingenuous; if they did find

Ulmil Pavilion atop Mt. Kumsu and,
on the hillside, the temple where juvenile
Qilin romped; if we learned the unicorn

was, or is, the Qilin's more homely kin;
if the skeptics renounced their logic
and we demanded more colorful lies.

Bathos

The domestic stage does not diminish the tragedy,
at least for the players. One can see, then, the dry

jet tub as war's bright theatre, its deep white bowl
a boneyard littered with hard dark carcasses.

The few survivors, visible in dawn's light film, twitch
on the plain above which a massacre played out in the night,

the largest a limping cricket. They must have negotiated
the tear in the screen and by chance or hunch escaped the web.

Tucked now in her tunnel's dim lace, itself funneled
in the nozzle's cave, the spider spent the morning rappelling

to the basin's smooth deck, climbing again, trailing silk
with each pass and now again awaits the hysterias

of the newly doomed. Some odd courtesy urges me to sweep
the dead from the field, dismantle the lair, and crush

its terrible occupant. But her venom serves me well. She keeps
the afternoon's hatch from its lamp-fueled mania,

from plundering the enameled canyons floored with my gums
as I sleep through the night, slack-jawed and oblivious.

And We Question the Will of the Sullen

Her elbows prick the Buick's hood.
One palm cups her face, and the weight
of the day is apparent by noon.

Dirty blond bangs strain the plume
rising straight from the tip of her fifth
Camel Light. Runoff, festooned by oil

and gas, passes her feet before pouring
over the iron bit of the grate and into
the darkness harnessed there. The boy

hoists grocery bags from the cart, flings
them into the trunk as if the thought of
food repulses him. Inside, by the case

displaying the trove of pot pies, he had
pointed to a chicken box, a beef one,
and then to a turkey pie bulging with

mushrooms and peas. Betrayed by
variety, he could not choose beneath
the boiling cumulus of his mother's scowl.

The hickory switch she'd smuggled in
arced parallel to the floor, perpendicular
to the bare white bars of his shins,

and pink ropes threaded his skin.
Shoppers slowed, pushed on.
From the boy, not a sound. He looked

straight at his mother when she was
spent, then shoved the cart toward
the milk. Outside, Muzak spurts

from the store's sliding doors.
In the asphalt air of Allendale,
all kinds of pain melt in the heat.

Gentle Slaughter

The women and liberated men thumping melons
at Whole Foods this year require chickens
labeled *gently slaughtered,* meaning rendered
insensible before their throats were cut.

Syglenda has obliged them and opened a shed
where the birds are gassed before uncrating,
before exsanguination. She knows how Tyson
shackles them upside down on a belt that draws

them through an electrical bath before they reach
the blade and the vat, how they sometimes jerk,
miss the shock and reach the scald alert.
She remembers her mother sitting in the shade,

whetting a knife while hens scuttled at her feet.
Pulling the knife along the stone, she sang lullabies
to calm the birds. Syglenda considers the physics
of wringing chicken necks—the grip, the opposing

twists of the wrists, the torque. She recalls a headless
hen scuffing up dust and her father not leaving the field
until finding the wing-shot dove, slapping its head
against his heel to be sure that it was dead.

Acknowledgments

The author gratefully acknowledges the editors of the following publications in which the poems listed first appeared, sometimes in different form:

2River View: "Elsewhere" and "Eric with Spike the Rooster 2001"

Appalachian Heritage: "Aviary"

Apple Valley Review: "Renaissance Man"

Asheville Poetry Review: "Gentle Slaughter"

Avatar Review: "Exodus," "Qilin," and "The Lesson"

Bayou Magazine: "Preserved"

Ekphrasis: "Memoir" (as "The Subject Defines Itself")

Fourteen Hills: The San Francisco State University Review: "Bird in Hand" and "Slur"

Free Lunch: "The Vicar"

Fugue: "Donnie with Baby and Cows 1999"

Furman Magazine: "Another Good Morning" (originally in *Valparaiso Poetry Review*)

Iodine Poetry Journal: "Inquisition" (as "Progeny") and "Prelude to a Hunt" (as "Prelude to a Hunt, 1967")

Juxtaprose Literary Magazine: "Dead of Winter"

One: "Not Quite Sisyphus"

Passages North: "Bait"

Redux: "Fear of Giants" (originally in *Shenandoah*)

Shenandoah: "Fear of Giants" and "New Year, White County, Arkansas"

South Dakota Review: "Beatitude"

Southeast Review: "I Spent Most of Elementary School Fearing Quicksand" and "To Dr. Paulson on the Eve of Surgery"

Southern Humanities Review: "Luminary" and "Ode to the God of Dogs"

Stone River Sky: An Anthology of Georgia Poems: "It's Pronounced [**tree-u**ʰ *n*]"

The Bitter Southerner: "Otherwise Gentle"

Valparaiso Poetry Review: "Another Good Morning"

About the Author

PHILIP BELCHER is the Vice President of Programs for The Community Foundation of Western North Carolina in Asheville and the author of *The Flies and Their Lovely Names*, selected by Kwame Dawes as the winner of the South Carolina Poetry Initiative chapbook prize and published by Stepping Stones Press. A graduate of Furman University, Southeastern Baptist Theological Seminary (M.Div.), and Duke University School of Law (JD), he also earned an MFA in Poetry from Converse College and is the recipient of both the Porter Fleming Prize in Poetry and *Shenandoah*'s Carter Prize for the Essay. Belcher's poems and critical prose have appeared in numerous journals, including *The Southeast Review*, *Shenandoah*, *Southern Humanities Review*, *Passages North*, *Fugue*, *The Southern Quarterly*, and *Asheville Poetry Review*. He also served as an Advisory and Contributing Editor for *Shenandoah*.

www.ingramcontent.com/pod-product-compliance
Lightning Source LLC
Chambersburg PA
CBHW020336170426
43200CB00006B/399